Sponges

by Colleen Sexton

BELLWETHER MEDIA · MINNEAPOLIS, MN

Note to Librarians, Teachers, and Parents:

Blastoff! Readers are carefully developed by literacy experts and combine standards-based content with developmentally appropriate text.

Level 1 provides the most support through repetition of high-frequency words, light text, predictable sentence patterns, and strong visual support.

Level 2 offers early readers a bit more challenge through varied simple sentences, increased text load, and less repetition of high-frequency words.

Level 3 advances early-fluent readers toward fluency through increased text and concept load, less reliance on visuals, longer sentences, and more literary language.

Level 4 builds reading stamina by providing more text per page, increased use of punctuation, greater variation in sentence patterns, and increasingly challenging vocabulary.

Level 5 encourages children to move from "learning to read" to "reading to learn" by providing even more text, varied writing styles, and less familiar topics.

Whichever book is right for your reader, Blastoff! Readers are the perfect books to build confidence and encourage a love of reading that will last a lifetime!

This edition first published in 2010 by Bellwether Media, Inc.

No part of this publication may be reproduced in whole or in part without written permission of the publisher. For information regarding permission, write to Bellwether Media, Inc., Attention: Permissions Department, Post Office Box 19349, Minneapolis, MN 55419.

Library of Congress Cataloging-in-Publication Data
Sexton, Colleen A., 1967-
 Sponges / by Colleen Sexton.
   p. cm. – (Blastoff! readers. Oceans alive)
 Includes bibliographical references and index.
 Summary: "Simple text and full color photographs introduce beginning readers to sponges. Developed by literacy experts for students in kindergarten through third grade"–Provided by publisher.
 ISBN 978-1-60014-268-0 (hardcover : alk. paper)
 1. Sponges–Juvenile literature. I. Title.

 QL371.6.S48 2009
 593.4-dc22
                      2009008480

Contents

Sponges are animals. They live in every ocean in the world.

They live in shallow places
and deep places.

There are more than 5,000
different kinds of sponges.

Some sponges are as small as the tip of a pencil. Some are bigger than a person.

Sponges come in many shapes.
They can look like tubes, fans,
vases, cups, or barrels.

Sponges come in many colors.
They can be yellow, purple,
orange, gray, or brown.

Sponges stick to rocks, **reefs**, and other objects on the ocean floor.

10

Some sponges grow close together in a group. They look like one giant sponge!

11

Most sponges stay in one
place all their lives.

Some sponges stick to the **shells** of snails, crabs, and other animals. These sponges go places!

A sponge does not have a heart, a stomach, or a brain. It does not have a head, mouth, eyes, or ears.

Sponges have hard **skeletons**.
The skeletons are made of thick
threads or sharp spikes.

Sponges have tough skin outside their skeletons.

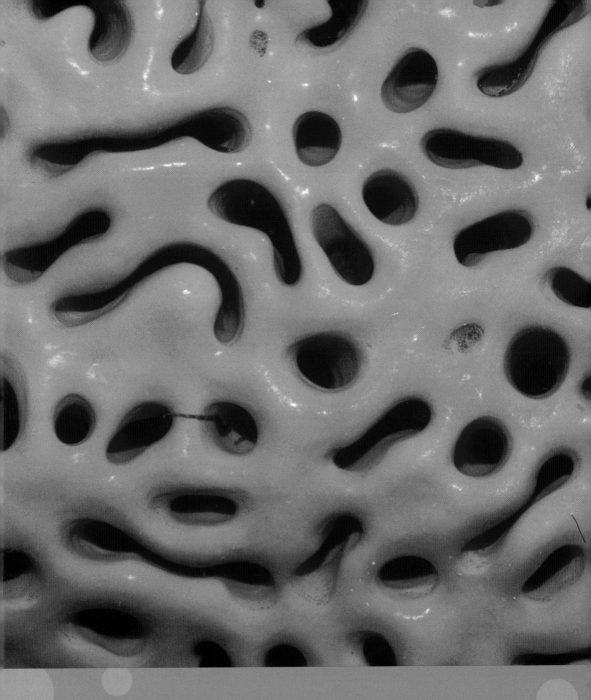

Small holes cover a sponge's body. Water flows into the holes.

The water carries in tiny plants and animals. They are food for sponges.

Water flows out through a
large hole.

Water moves in and out of sponges. Sponges are **filters**. They take **bacteria** out of the water.

Sponges help keep ocean
waters clean!

Glossary

bacteria—tiny living things that cannot be seen with the human eye; some bacteria carry diseases that can harm plants and animals.

filter—a part of an animal that lets water pass through but catches small bits of food and bacteria

reef—a ridge of rock or coral near the surface of the water

shell—the hard covering on the outside of an animal's body

skeleton—the hard parts that make up the frame of an animal's body

To Learn More

AT THE LIBRARY

Coldiron, Deborah. *Sea Sponges*. Edina, Minn.:
ABDO, 2007.

Esbensen, Barbara Juster. *Sponges Are Skeletons*.
New York, N.Y.: HarperCollins, 1993.

Lunis, Natalie. *Squishy Sponges*. New York, N.Y.:
Bearport, 2007.

ON THE WEB

Learning more about sponges
is as easy as 1, 2, 3.

1. Go to www.factsurfer.com.

2. Enter "sponges" into the search box.

3. Click the "Surf" button and you will see a list of
    related Web sites.

With factsurfer.com, finding more information is just a
click away.

Index

The images in this book are reproduced through the courtesy of: Marsha Goldenberg, front cover, p. 19; Dennis Sabo, pp. 4-5; Brandon Cole, pp. 6, 14-15; Durden Images, p. 7; Jeff Hunter / Getty Images, pp. 8, 20-21; Stephen Frink Collection / Alamy, p. 9; John Anderson, p. 10; WaterFrame / Alamy, p. 11; imagebroker / Alamy, p. 12; Wolfgang Pölzer / Alamy, p. 13; Masa Ushioda / imagequestmarine.com, p. 16; Roger Steene / imagequestmarine.com, p. 17; John A. Anderson, p. 18.